Anchored

Finding Strength in Your Struggles

Johnny L. Moore III

ISBN-13: 978-1-954609-81-5

For information regarding special discounts for bulk purchases, please contact the publisher: LaBoo Publishing Enterprise, LLC

staff@laboopublishing.com
www.laboopublishing.com

Printed in the United States of America

Dedication

To Johnny Moore IV a.k.a. Joe, "Daddy's Man, 100 Grand"

Joe, I wrote this book with you in mind—not just for the man you'll become, but for the boy you are now. You're amazing in my eyes, already full of intellect, wit, wonder, strength, and purpose. One day, life will surely test you. Struggles will come in your life—some loud and some silent. In those moments, I pray you'll remember that your strength doesn't come from yourself alone, but from the God who formed you, walks with you, and will never leave you.

I pray you will never question your faith in Him, even when the storms of life blow violently and the ground beneath you feels unsteady. I pray that you will trust God when the direction you are to take is unclear and the decision you must make is unpopular. I pray that you will always find hope when life gets heavy. My greatest hope is that you'll handle your struggles better than I ever did—not by being perfect, but by being real, humble, and anchored in the truth of God's Word.

When you're tempted to give up, I pray you'll press on. When you feel weak, I pray you'll lean into the strength of God. And when you doubt your worth in this world, I pray you'll remember you are deeply loved by your heavenly Father—and by me. As I write this book, you are just starting kindergarten, but I pray that these scriptures and prayers will strengthen, encourage, and guide you for the rest of your life.

I love you more than life itself, Joe. Being your dad is the greatest honor and responsibility I've ever known. I'm always here to offer strength to you for every struggle you will face in life. You'll always be My Man, 100 grand!

Have I not commanded you? Be strong and courageous. Do not be afraid; do not be discouraged, for the Lord your God will be with you wherever you go. —Joshua 1:9

With all my heart,

Daddy

INTRODUCTION

Life as a man comes with a unique set of pressures and silent battles—anxiety, self-doubt, insecurity, financial stress, depression, and the unrelenting expectation to always be strong. But what if true strength isn't found in pretending to have it all together, but in learning to lean on the One who holds it all together?

Anchored: Finding Strength in Your Struggles is a 30-day devotional designed specifically for men who are walking through hard places and looking for hope. Each day offers a focused scripture, a powerful devotion rooted in real-life challenges, a reflection question for honest self-examination, and a heartfelt prayer to help you connect with God in the midst of life's battles.

Whether you're battling internal struggles or external pressures, this devotional reminds you that God doesn't abandon men in their weakness—He meets them there. Whether you're trying to overcome fear and insecurity or struggling to reclaim your identity and purpose, God is here.

Are you seeking to rediscover courage and find peace? These daily devotions will help you break the silence around your struggle and find strength in the presence of a faithful God. You don't have to carry the weight alone. You were never meant to. God wants to strengthen you in every struggle you currently face.

This is more than a devotional—it's a daily invitation to rebuild you as a man from the inside out. It will walk you through the process of renewing your confidence and reassure you that you are not forgotten, disqualified, or too far gone. You are called, equipped, and strengthened, even in the struggle.

Let God remind you who you are. Let Him strengthen you, one day at a time.

Anchored

Finding Strength in Your Struggles

Day 1:
You Are Not What You've Done

Scripture: 2 Corinthians 5:17 - *"Therefore, if anyone is in Christ, the new creation has come: The old has gone, the new is here!"*

Devotional: Men, hear this—your past mistakes don't define your future. As men, we often carry the weight of our past like a backpack full of bricks. Bricks labeled failures, regrets, and broken promises. When we come to Jesus, He makes us into a brand-new creation—one that bears no resemblance to the old you. God is not at all interested in who you were. He's invested in shaping who you are becoming. We are often taught that our identity, as men, is rooted in our performance. That can't be further from the truth. As followers of Christ, our identity is found solely in His grace.

Reflection Question: What is one label or failure from your past that you need to surrender to God today?

_____

_____

_____

Prayer: Lord, thank You that, in Christ, I am a new creation. Help me to release the shame of my past and embrace the identity You've given me. Amen.

Day 2:
Son, Not Servant

Scripture: Romans 8:15 "The Spirit you received does not make you slaves, so that you live in fear again; rather, the Spirit you received brought about your adoption to sonship."

Devotional: As men, we sometimes approach God like fearful servants and not His sons. Many of us have been told we must work harder and do more to be accepted by God. This misconception must be debunked—you are already accepted by God. You've been adopted into God's family, not as a distant cousin, but as a full son. And being a son gives you full access to your Father. Let this truth bring you security—security that overrides all the shame you've ever felt. The goal is to exude confidence, not fear. Our confidence must be anchored in our relationship with God, our Father.

Reflection Question: Do you relate to God more like a son or a servant? Why?

Prayer: Lord, thank You for viewing me as a son and giving me access to You as my father. Help me to always walk in boldness and confidence, secure in my identity as Your son. Remind me daily of how you view me—not how I see myself. Thank you for choosing me to be a part of your family. Amen.

Day 3:
You Were Created with Purpose

Scripture: Ephesians 2:10 – "For we are God's masterpiece. He has created us anew in Christ Jesus, so we can do the good things He planned for us long ago."

Devotional: Men, we were created for a purpose. You were not an accident. Even if you weren't a part of your parents' plans, you were always a part of God's plan—He made you with a plan in mind. We all face chaotic times in life. Remember that you are a masterpiece in progress. That means your worth is not based on your bank account, job title, or physical strength. Your value is inextricably tied to the One who created you—and He doesn't make mistakes. The path to discovering your purpose can only be found in God.

Reflection Question: What lies have you believed about your worth that go against God's truth?

_____

_____

_____

Prayer: God, thank You for reminding me that I am Your master-piece. With all of my undeniable flaws and failures, help me see myself the way You see me. Amen.

Day 4:
Finding Strength in Weakness

Scripture: 2 Corinthians 12:9 – "My grace is sufficient for you, for my power is made perfect in weakness."

Devotional: Real strength isn't shown by pretending you have it all together. Real strength is found in the humility to admit your places of weakness and your need for God. When you feel like you're inadequate, know that God is more than sufficient. We often hide our weaknesses out of fear that they make us seem less than a man. But God says it's in our weakness that His power is best seen. Let your weakness become your pathway to experiencing His strength in every part of your life.

Reflection Question: Where do you feel weak right now? How do you think God wants to show His strength in that area of your life?

_____

_____

_____

Prayer: Jesus, I give You my weaknesses. Use them to reveal Your power in my life. Help me see my weaknesses as a chance to experience Your strength. Amen.

Day 5:
You Are Known and Loved

Scripture: Psalm 139:1 – "You have searched me, Lord, and you know me."

Devotional: My brother, God knows everything about you—your thoughts, your fears, your flaws. And yes, He still loves you. You don't have to hide from Him. Many men wrestle with being fully known, fearing rejection if someone sees the real them. With God, you are fully known and fully loved. He doesn't seek to judge you for who you are or what you've done. Your mistakes don't disqualify you from His love, care, and concern for you. The foundation of confidence and healing for every man is rooted in this truth—God knows you and loves you unconditionally.

Reflection Question: What parts of yourself have you been afraid to let God into?

_____

_____

Prayer: Father, thank You for knowing us completely and still loving us. Help us live in the freedom of this truth. Let the reassurance of Your love prompt us to become the men You created us to be. Amen.

Day 6:
You Reflect God's Image

Scripture: Genesis 1:27 – "So God created mankind in his own image... male and female he created them."

Devotional: Man, do you know you carry the image of the Creator of the universe? Just as your son may reflect your personality or features, we reflect the image of our Father. Deeper than physical traits, you were designed with dignity, value, and the divine imprint of God. The world often tries to define you by your failures, your looks, or your accomplishments. But your identity is already established—you were wonderfully made in God's image. Walk like it. Live like it. Talk like it. Lead like it. Love like it.

Reflection Question: What would change in your life if you truly believed you were made in God's image?

_____

_____

_____

_____

Prayer: Lord, remind us daily that we carry Your image. Let that truth shape how we live, lead, and love. Amen.

Day 7:
Rooted in Christ, Not Comparison

Scripture: Galatians 6:4 – "Each one should test their own actions. Then they can take pride in themselves alone, without comparing themselves to someone else."

Devotional: Comparison is a thief that robs men of their joy, peace, and purpose. When you measure your worth against another man's success or strength, you lose sight of your own. God made every man unique. You don't need to copy anyone else. Be yourself—everyone else is taken. Stay focused on your identity in Christ and let Him define your success according to His plan for your life.

Reflection Question: In what ways have you been comparing yourself to others?

_____

_____

_____

_____

Prayer: Jesus, keep me rooted and grounded in You and Your plan for my life. Help me stop comparing myself to others. Give me the courage and wisdom to live the life You've given me. Amen.

Day 8:

When Darkness Feels Closer Than Light

Scripture: Psalm 34:18 – "The Lord is close to the brokenhearted and saves those who are crushed in spirit."

Devotional: Man, depression is real. Your mental health should be a priority. Prioritizing your mental health doesn't make you weak—it makes you wise. You're human, living in a world full of problems we all experience. God doesn't push you away because you experience times of sadness—He draws closer to you. When you feel disappointed, undervalued, unappreciated, or uncertain about life, know that you're not alone. God's presence is not proven by the absence of pain, but by His comfort in the middle of it. For every real place of pain, there is a real God who loves you and will strengthen you through every difficulty you face.

Reflection Question: Where in your life do you feel broken or disappointed? How can you invite God into that space?

Prayer: God, I need You. Being a man sometimes makes others think I'm invincible. Lord, please meet me in my brokenness and remind me that I'm never alone. Surround me with positive people who will shine light in my dark places. Amen.

Day 9:
You Are Not a Burden

Scripture: Matthew 11:28 – "Come to me, all you who are weary and burdened, and I will give you rest."

Devotional: Sometimes the hardest thing for a man to say is, "I need help." Men, Jesus never sees your struggles as a burden to Him. You are not a nuisance to God because you share your troubles with Him. God desires that every weary man come to Him. God isn't looking to shame you for your mistakes or your current situation. God desires to see men restored to a place of health and wholeness. Your issues, cares, and concerns are never too much for God. You are not a burden to your Father. He's waiting for an opportunity to build a more meaningful relationship with His sons.

Reflection Question: What burden are you carrying alone that you need to bring to Jesus?

_____

_____

Prayer: Jesus, toDay I bring You the weight I've tried to carry alone. I can't do this on my own. While everyone may depend on me, I'm depending on You. Teach me to rest in You for all my needs. Amen.

Day 10:
It's Okay to Not Be Okay

Scripture: Ecclesiastes 3:4 – "A time to weep and a time to laugh, a time to mourn and a time to dance."

Devotional: Your faith in God doesn't mean you have to ignore the real pain you are feeling. Your faith is best seen when you learn to trust God with all of it. There are seasons that cause us to cry, but those times don't make us less of a man. A man's ability to express his emotions isn't a sign of weakness—it's proof of your humanity. God allows men the space to grieve so He can bring healing to those dark areas.

Reflection Question: Are you allowing yourself to feel and process the pain you carry? What positive outlets are you currently using to process the vicissitudes of life'?

_____

_____

_____

Prayer: Father, help me be honest with my emotions and allow You to heal my wounds. Give me a community of men I can trust to support me and hold me accountable. Amen.

Day 11:
Faith Over Feelings

Scripture: 2 Corinthians 5:7 – "For we live by faith, not by sight."

Devotional: Your feelings are real—but they aren't always reliable. Our faith is anchored in truth, not in our fleeting, wavering emotions. When fear, doubt, or discouragement rise up, we must decide to be led by what God says instead of what we feel in the moment. Feelings can distort our view of reality, but our faith in God offers a positive perspective. We must think, speak, and respond according to God's perspective—not external influences. Let your reality be filtered by faith and not your limited sight.

Reflection Question: How have your feelings been dictating your decisions? What can you do to start letting your faith lead instead?

_____

_____

_____

Prayer: Lord, strengthen my faith. Help me trust Your Word over my emotions. When I struggle to let go, remind me to lean on You and remember I can trust You, even in places that feel void of Your presence. My faith, trust, and hope are in You. Amen.

Day 12:
Courage to Begin Again

Scripture: Isaiah 43:19 – "See, I am doing a new thing! Now it springs up; do you not perceive it?"

Devotional: The failures you've experienced don't mean it's over with God. Every ending in your life marks the beginning of something new. At times, we're paralyzed by the shadow of our past failures. That paralysis can cause us to doubt our ability to bounce back to where we know we're meant to be. Fear is a normal emotion—it's only harmful when we let it stop us from starting something new. The presence of courage isn't the absence of fear; it's choosing to move forward in spite of it. God specializes in giving fresh starts. Start today with a fresh perspective and trust God with your next step.

Reflection Question: What new beginning is God inviting you to step into today? What specific fears are preventing you from moving forward?

Prayer: Father, give me the strength, courage, and resilience to embrace the new things You are doing in my life. Help me feel the fear—and move forward anyway. Amen.

Day 13:
Anchored in His Promises

Scripture: Hebrews 10:23 – "Let us hold unswervingly to the hope we profess, for he who promised is faithful."

Devotional: God's promises are not based on your performance but on His faithfulness. The pressure is off—you don't have to be perfect to experience the grace of a perfect God. When you anchor yourself in His Word, you can stand firm even when the winds and rain of life try to beat you down. His promises don't guarantee a life without storms, but they do give assurance that we will survive.

Reflection Question: What promise of God do you need to hold onto today?

_____

_____

_____

_____

Prayer: God, help me stand firm on Your promises—even when I can't see immediate results. The storms I face may be blinding, but I trust Your faithfulness will get me through every storm as promised. Amen.

Day 14:
Restoring What Was Broken

Scripture: Joel 2:25 – "I will restore to you the years that the swarming locust has eaten."

Devotional: God is not only the healer of hearts—He's also the restorer of lost time. Sometimes we look back and see how we've wasted precious time and resources. We tend to focus on how those decisions caused setbacks in certain areas of our lives. God is not one-dimensional in His ability to heal—He also restores. Even when we make mistakes that seem irreversible, God can redeem us and rebuild the places in our lives that were destroyed. Nothing is too broken for His hands. It's only when we put it in His hands that true restoration will take place.

Reflection Question: Where do you need to trust God to bring restoration?

Prayer: Lord, I believe You can redeem my brokenness. Please restore what has been lost as a result of my decisions. I know You can make up the time that I lost. Restore my heart, my mind, my hope, my joy, and my vision for my future. Amen.

Day 15:

When You Feel Overlooked

Scripture: Galatians 6:9 – "Let us not become weary in doing good, for at the proper time we will reap a harvest if we do not give up."

Devotional: As men, we juggle many roles and responsibilities in life. Our quest to be the best in every part of life is not always met with acknowledgment or appreciation. Sometimes we feel overlooked by family, friends, and colleagues. But being unseen by people doesn't mean you're unseen by God. Your faithfulness to those who depend on you is never wasted. Keep showing up. Keep leading. Keep loving. Keep grinding. Keep serving. Your harvest of fulfillment and contentment is coming.

Reflection Question: In what areas of life do you struggle to keep doing good? How do you handle the thoughts and feelings of being overlooked?

_____

_____

Prayer: Father, strengthen me to keep going—even when no one sees but You. Let my motivation to be the best man I can be come from the impact I have on the lives of others. Thank you for seeing me and caring about me. Amen.

Day 16:
Freedom from Shame

Scripture: Romans 8:1 – "Therefore, there is now no condemnation for those who are in Christ Jesus."

Devotional: We all have a past filled with decisions and actions we aren't proud of. You are not what you've done. When we sulk too long over our shameful past, it often whispers to us that we are disqualified. Shame has a way of making us feel unworthy—and sometimes like we deserve a tumultuous life. But Jesus says you are redeemed, forgiven, and worthy of living life free from shame. Don't allow shame to write your story—let grace do that instead. Walk in the freedom that's yours in Jesus Christ.

Reflection Question: What mistakes haunt you the most? What will help you release the shame and receive God's grace?

_____

_____

_____

Prayer: Lord, I choose Your forgiveness over my shame. Help me to walk in a new chapter of life—one that exudes confidence in who You are and how You see me. Thank you for reassuring me of Your love and the forgiveness You have for me. Amen.

Day 17:
Turning Fear Into Fuel

Scripture: 2 Timothy 1:7 – "For God gave us a spirit not of fear but of power and love and self-control."

Devotional: Some cars rely on gasoline to fuel their engines—this ensures the car will get you to your desired destination. I learned the hard way that putting the wrong fuel in the gas tank can cause costly problems—stalling the car and not reaching its potential. Unfortunately, many men use fear to fuel their decisions in life. In doing so, we never reach our full potential. Fear is a natural emotion—but if it's not channeled in the proper way, it can cause paralysis. Our true destination in life should be to get closer to God. Fear causes us to second-guess the greatest decision a man can make—giving his life to God. Men, we must resolve to fuel ourselves on faith and not fear. Faith fuels our trust in God in every area of our lives. It allows us to feel the fear but go for it anyway. It's not too late to change what fuels you. Choose FAITH over FEAR.

Reflection Question: What part of your life has been consumed by fear? Are you willing to turn it over to God today?

_____

_____

Prayer: God, give us the courage to turn our fear into faith. Fill me with power, love, and discipline. Let us be led by faith in every decision ahead of us. Strengthen us in areas of our lives where fear has paralyzed us. We trust You, and we exercise our faith in You today. Amen.

Day 18:
Forgiving Yourself

Scripture: Psalm 103:12 – "As far as the east is from the west, so far has he removed our transgressions from us."

Devotional: Man, God has forgiven you. Knowing all the wrong things that we have done, it can be hard to grasp the notion that God really forgives us. God not only knows what you've done—your mistakes never caught him by surprise. He forgives you and doesn't dwell on your past. And as if believing that God has forgiven us weren't hard enough, we must also learn to forgive ourselves. Friends, family, coworkers, associates, fraternity brothers and—even society—may never truly forgive us. But we can't base our ability to forgive ourselves on whether others choose to hold our past over our heads. Free yourself from the figurative jail sentence you've imposed on yourself for past mistakes. Forgive yourself—starting today. Own your mistakes, repent, set boundaries to avoid repeating those actions, and move on. Your future will never be fully embraced while holding on to the guilt of your past. God sees you past your mistakes and shortcomings. Now it's time to agree with His view of you—and stop holding onto what God has already erased.

Reflection Question: What forgiveness do you need to extend to yourself today?

_____

_____

Prayer: Lord, teach me to walk in the freedom of Your forgiveness. I repent for what I've done wrong—to you and to others. I want to be a better man, and a better me is a free me. Thank you for Your forgiveness and the unconditional love You have for me. Amen.

Day 19:
Stay Anchored When Life Shakes You

Scripture: Matthew 7:24 – "Everyone who hears these words of mine and puts them into practice is like a wise man who built his house on the rock."

Devotional: Storms are inevitable. Collapse is not. Disappointment will happen. Sulking is an option. Bad times are guaranteed. But bad perspectives? That's a choice—a convenient one for a man with a toolbox of excuses. A wise man doesn't try to avoid the inevitable but builds himself and his surroundings to withstand it. Bad things happen to good people. Great men survive them and then teach others how to do the same. God doesn't love you any less because He allows you to face storms. No storm lasts forever—and each one carries a lesson to be learned. Don't anchor your life in things that are fleeting or wavering. Anchor yourself in the strong foundation of God's Word, where you will find His promises for life's tumultuous times. Stay anchored in Christ, and you'll stand firm.

Reflection Question: What foundation are you building your life on today?

Prayer: Jesus, be the foundation I can stand on. Provide me with wisdom, protect me from reckless thinking, and keep me centered in Your plan for my life. Strengthen my foundation. Amen.

Day 20:
Building Strength Daily

Scripture: Luke 16:10 – "Whoever can be trusted with very little can also be trusted with much."

Devotional: Our strength—in every part of life—is built through small, daily choices. Our consistency matters much more than intensity. It's nearly impossible to increase the weights you lift in the gym from week to week if you work out only once a week. You can't lift 145 pounds one week and jump to 225 the next without building up your strength in between. Real progress comes from our relentless effort to master the weight of the day. When we master today's weight, we are better prepared to handle the weight of tomorrow. Build your faith, peace, and future—one Day at a time.

Reflection Question: What small habit can you start toDay that will build lasting strength?

Prayer: God, help me be faithful in the small things. Let me give my best every Day as I build strength to be the man You desire me to be. Amen.

Day 21:
Listening for God's Voice

Scripture: John 10:27 – "My sheep listen to my voice; I know them, and they follow me."

Devotional: Many ask, "Does God still speak?" The answer is an emphatic yes. He speaks to us daily in so many ways. He may not speak in an audible voice, but He still speaks—subtly and consistently, like the GPS does in your car. God leads His people in the direction He wants us to go. The real question is—are we listening to His voice? Are we ignoring His daily promptings and warnings? Do we truly value hearing His voice and following His direction for our lives? Be intentional—make space to listen.

Reflection Question: What distractions do you need to silence in your life to hear God more clearly?

_____

_____

_____

Prayer: Lord, open my ears to hear Your voice. Help me to quiet the noise in my life so I can prioritize hearing from You every day. Amen.

Day 22:
A Purposeful Pursuit

Scripture: Proverbs 21:21 – "Whoever pursues righteousness and love finds life, prosperity and honor."

Devotional: Our society celebrates the loud success of prosperity and fame. God honors the quiet pursuit of purpose through faithfulness. Living without true love and a relationship with God means living beneath the privilege God gives every man. God isn't opposed to you being wealthy—but He doesn't want you to pursue it at the cost of wealth and struggle in your relationship with Him. The goal of our pursuit should be anchored in our love for God and our relationship with Him. Chasing tangible things means focusing on temporary things—things that will quickly fade. But pursuing peace, joy, love, and contentment is rooted in our God-given purpose. Let's be honest—we all know men with expensive cars, clothes, and notoriety. But the truth be told, having those things doesn't always bring peace, joy, or contentment. Having more doesn't mean living with peace—but peace and joy give you what you need to live as a successful man, no matter what you lack.

Reflection Question: How can you begin to pursue purpose? What brings you peace, joy, and contentment?

Prayer: Lord, help us live a life filled with the pursuit of Your purpose. Surround us with men who will help us stay on track and focused on our pursuits. Amen.

Day 23:
You Are Equipped

Scripture: 2 Peter 1:3 – "His divine power has given us everything we need for a godly life."

Devotional: One of the most common struggles men face is the idea that they don't have what it takes to succeed. Be assured—whatever God has called you to be in life, He's given you what you need to attain it. You are wired uniquely and intentionally for a life that is driven by purpose. Your unique gifts and talents were given to you before you even knew what to do with them. Your metaphorical toolbox is already filled with the character traits and equipment you need to get to where God predestined you to go. The challenge is to trust His provision—and believe that you have what it takes to be the man God created you to be.

Reflection Question: In what area of life do you need to trust that God has already equipped you?

_____

_____

Prayer: Lord, thank You for reminding me that You've already given me everything I need. Help me believe that I lack nothing in You. Teach me to use the equipment you have given me wisely, for your glory. Amen.

Day 24:
Guard Your Heart

Scripture: Proverbs 4:23 – "Above all else, guard your heart, for everything you do flows from it."

Devotional: As men, we go to great lengths to protect what we consider valuable—our homes, cars, spouses, family members, and more. But let me ask you this: What are you doing to guard your heart? I know that might seem more like an exercise in femininity but let me assure you that it's a necessary discipline for every man. Your heart holds your perspective and emotions, and that makes it one of the most important parts of who you are. The way you think about yourself shapes the way you treat yourself—and also how you treat others. Your heart is the wellspring of your life. So guard it. Guard it from bitterness. From cynicism. From distraction. Guard your heart like your life depends on it—because it truly does.

Reflection Question: What negative influences do you need to guard against today?

_____

_____

Prayer: Father, help me guard my heart with Your wisdom. Help me discern the negative influences and distractions that inhibit my growth. Be the ultimate protector of my heart and keep me focused on the path to becoming a better man. Amen.

Day 25:
The Battle Belongs to the Lord

Scripture: 2 Chronicles 20:15 – "The battle is not yours, but God's."

Devotional: All men are wired to be protectors, and with that wiring comes both a propensity and a responsibility to fight for what is assigned to our care. But that natural inclination can sometimes lead us to handle too much on our own. Our unwillingness to relinquish control—especially in situations marked by hardship, hurt, anger, or disappointment—can stop us from experiencing victory over those things. But the truth is that these battles are won by the omnipotence of God. You are not fighting alone. Give the battle back to God.

Reflection Question: What fight do you need to give to the Lord?

_____

_____

_____

_____

_____

Prayer: God, toDay I give this battle to you. It's Yours now. Strengthen my ability to trust you with every battle I face. Amen.

Day 26:
Speak Life

Scripture: Proverbs 18:21 – "The tongue has the power of life and death."

Devotional: Men, we must recognize the weight of our words. Often, our environment is a direct result of what we have said. We have the power to kill what's living—and breathe life into what's dead. We should be resolved to speak only hope, faith, and encouragement—over ourselves and others. Utilizing the authority God has given us authority to speak life, and that carries a great responsibility. Steward your words well and watch what you speak over grow immensely.

Reflection Question: Who needs to hear life-giving words from you today? What area in your life can you speak life into that needs to be resuscitated?

_____

_____

_____

Prayer: Jesus, let my words reflect Your desire and destiny for my life. Help me reject negativity and embrace the authority that I possess in the words that you've given me to speak. Let my words lead to lasting impact—in my life and the lives of others. Amen.

Day 27:
Anchored in Hope

Scripture: Romans 15:13 – "May the God of hope fill you with all joy and peace as you trust in him."

Devotional: Hope is not just wishful thinking. Our hope is anchored in God's unchanging nature. When we choose to anchor our hope in God, we declare that He is worthy of our trust. Trusting someone with our hope means believing in their ability to meet our needs. God has proven Himself worthy of our hope. We must resist the temptation to pull our hope away from Him when we encounter inevitable problems. Hope in God doesn't erase the likelihood of bad things happening—it gives us faith that hardship won't bring our demise. Keep hope alive in Jesus—and trust that life will work out the way He intends it to.

Reflection Question: How can you anchor yourself more deeply in hope today?

_____

_____

Prayer: Father, fill me with Your unstoppable hope. Let the hope I have in You override the darkness of doubt and disbelief that I currently possess. I trust you to make all things work together for our betterment. Amen.

Day 28:
Struggles With Anxiety

Scripture: *"Cast all your anxiety on him because he cares for you."* — 1 Peter 5:7

Devotion: Anxiety can feel like an insurmountable struggle in your mind. It builds pressure that you can't release. Often, men don't even know the origin of this emotion. As a man, you might feel ashamed—afraid that others might see it as weakness. But let me boldly tell you—you don't have to struggle with this alone. God doesn't want us to carry anxiety. He wants us to release it to Him. And it isn't a one-time event. It's a daily, sometimes hourly, act of surrender.

Reflection Question: What's one anxious thought you can release to God today? What's stopping you from doing it?

_____

_____

_____

Prayer: God, sometimes we feel overwhelmed with anxiety. We've tried to hide it, suppress it, and fight it—but it keeps rising up. Help me trust You enough to let it go. As often as it returns, give me the courage to release it to you. Remind me that You care about me and my mental health. I'm not alone. Amen.

Day 29:

Built for More

Scripture: *"Have I not commanded you? Be strong and courageous. Do not be afraid; do not be discouraged, for the Lord your God will be with you wherever you go."* — Joshua 1:9

Devotion: Some days, life hits men hard. Our responsibilities pile up, confidence runs low, and it feels like we're merely surviving. As men, we often question whether we're enough—for our family, our work, and our calling. Joshua 1:9 is a powerful reminder to men that you we were built for more than fear and discouragement. God doesn't suggest that we exhibit courage—He commands it. Not because you can possess courage on your own, but because God is with you. His presence changes everything. You're not fighting for victory—you're fighting *from* it. God is with you—and that makes you stronger than you know.

Reflection Question: Where in your life do you need to step out in courage?

Prayer: Father, thank You for reminding me that I don't face life's battles alone. When fear and discouragement weigh me down, remind me that You are with me. Give me the courage to keep showing up—and faith to believe You're working things out for me. Amen.

Day 30:
Finish Strong

Scripture: 2 Timothy 4:7 – "I have fought the good fight, I have finished the race, I have kept the faith."

Devotional: God doesn't just want us to start well—He wants us to finish strong. We must keep fighting the good fight. Your story matters. Your spouse, your children, and your friends depend on your perseverance. The race is not over—and when fatigue and exhaustion set in, God will give you a second wind. Don't quit. Finish strong.

Reflection Question: What will it take for you to finish this season strong?

_____

_____

_____

_____

_____

Prayer: Lord, strengthen my mind and heart for the final stretch. Help me finish strong in You. Amen.

Notes

Notes

Notes

Notes

Notes

Notes

Notes

Notes

Notes

Notes

Notes

Notes

Notes

Notes

_____

_____

_____

_____

_____

_____

_____

_____

_____

_____

_____

_____

_____

_____

Notes

Notes

Notes

Notes

Notes

Notes

_____

_____

_____

_____

_____

_____

_____

_____

_____

_____

_____

_____

_____

www.ingramcontent.com/pod-product-compliance
Lightning Source LLC
LaVergne TN
LVHW051203080426
835508LV00021B/2778